Collins

11+
Verbal
Reasoning

Quick Practice Tests
Ages 9-10

Flora MacInnes

Contents

About this book

Familiarisation with 11+ test-style questions is a critical step in preparing your child for the 11+ selection tests. This book gives children lots of opportunities to test themselves in short, manageable bursts, helping to build confidence and improve the chance of test success.

It contains 60 tests designed to develop key verbal reasoning skills.

- Each test is designed to be completed within a short amount of time. Frequent, short bursts of revision are found to be more productive than lengthier sessions.

- GL Assessment tests can be quite time-pressured so these practice tests will help your child become accustomed to this style of questioning.

- We recommend your child uses a pencil to complete the tests, so that they can rub out the answers and try again at a later date if necessary.

- Children will need a pencil and a rubber to complete the tests as well as some spare paper for rough working. They will also need to be able to see a clock/watch and should have a quiet place in which to do the tests.

- Your child should **not** use a calculator for any of these tests.

- Answers to every question are provided at the back of the book, with explanations given where appropriate.

- After completing the tests, children should revisit their weaker areas and attempt to improve their scores and timings.

19.18
19:24

Code Sequences

You have 6 minutes to complete this test.

You have 10 questions to complete within the time given.

6

Use the alphabet below to help you with these questions.

A B C D E F G H I J K L M N O P Q R S T U V W X Y Z

In each question, write in the letters that are next in the sequence.

EXAMPLE

| FB | HB | JC | LC | ND | __PD__ |

---

(1)	JJ	LL	NN	PP	RR	TT
(2)	GA	HA	IB	JB	KC	LC
(3)	MV	NT	OR	PP	QN	RL
(4)	HB	GD	FF	EH	DJ	CL
(5)	PB	QB	RD	SD	TF	UF
(6)	AB	BC	CD	DE	EF	FG
(7)	JI	LJ	NK	PL	RM	TN
(8)	CZ	DZ	EY	FY	GX	HX
(9)	OB	PD	QF	RH	QJ	ST
(10)	PT	LW	HZ	DC	ZF	

Annotations on Q1: +2, +2, +2, +2, +2
Annotations on Q2: +1, +1, +1, +1

Score: .... / 10

4

Missing Letters

You have 6 minutes to complete this test.

You have 10 questions to complete within the time given.

In each question, three letters have been removed from the word in capitals.

These three letters correctly spell a new word without changing their order.

Write in the three missing letters.

EXAMPLE

BCH is a meal usually eaten from late morning to early afternoon. .... **RUN**

(*The word in capitals is BRUNCH.*)

(1) Richard finally switched off the COMER. .... *Put*

(2) The GORAS managed to escape their enclosure. .... *ril*

(3) PRACT makes perfect. .... *ice*

(4) The CHER had marked their homework. .... *tea*

(5) The old woman carried a bread BET. .... *ask*

(6) They always PED cards after dinner. .... *lay*

(7) Emily and her mother went grocery SHOPG. .... *Pin*

(8) Sarah added FL to her brownie mix. .... *our*

(9) Tread carefully! The floor is SPERY. .... *lip*

(10) Meg had a headache and a sore THR. .... *oat*

Score: .... / 10

19:25
19:26

Antonyms

You have 6 minutes to complete this test.

You have 10 questions to complete within the time given.

In each question, underline the two words (one from each group) that are most opposite in meaning.

(sad   last   bitter)

(tired   happy   friendly)

---

1 (ideal   innocent   winter)

(vision   sunshine   guilty)

2 (ignore   peace   nervous)

(relaxed   treaty   responsive)

3 (plain   wide   mud)

(clean   bald   narrow)

4 (wet   delicious   soup)

(coffee   tasteless   desert)

5 (wrinkled   lucky   hideous)

(unfortunate   watery   fashionable)

6 (deliberate   happy   attractive)

(better   good   unintentional)

7 (permanent   wild   brief)

(short   temporary   ignorant)

8 (steep   low   tomorrow)

(yesterday   hike   climb)

9 (strange   female   insect)

(ordinary   boyish   glad)

10 (energetic   angry   loud)

(charge   shy   lethargic)

Score: .... / 10

19:26
19:28

Related Words

You have 6 minutes to complete this test.

You have 10 questions to complete within the time given.

In each question, three of the words are related in some way.

Underline the two words that do not relate to the other three.

EXAMPLE

purple   <u>royal</u>   <u>fruit</u>   orange   grey

(The underlined words are not colours.)

(1) <u>keys</u>   piano   <u>pitch</u>   clarinet   banjo

(2) rake   trowel   bucket   <u>soil</u>   <u>shears</u>

(3) bracelet   <u>locket</u>   <u>wrist</u>   jewellery   brooch

(4) orchid   <u>field</u>   <u>garden</u>   sunflower   tulip

(5) tram   <u>wheel</u>   <u>transport</u>   bicycle   train

(6) castle   <u>princess</u>   <u>royal</u>   bungalow   cottage

(7) until   <u>over</u>   before   <u>under</u>   since

(8) liver   <u>skin</u>   kidney   <u>freckles</u>   intestine

(9) cube   <u>square</u>   pyramid   sphere   <u>triangle</u>

(10) <u>friend</u>   niece   <u>co-worker</u>   cousin   granddaughter

Score: .... / 10

Test	# Complete the Sum
5	You have 6 minutes to complete this test. You have 10 questions to complete within the time given.

In each question, write in the number that correctly completes the sum.

EXAMPLE

$3 + 9 = 6 +$ ___6___

---

(1) $13 + 2 \times 3 = 28 -$ ___9___

(2) $19 - (3 + 4) = 40 -$ ___28___

(3) $6 \times 5 - (3 + 12) = 3 \times$ ___5___

(4) $22 \times 3 + 1 = 25 +$ ___42___

$$\begin{array}{r} 67 \\ -25 \\ \hline 42 \end{array}$$

(5) $-6 + 5 \times 2 = -3 +$ ___1___

(6) $5 \times 9 - 29 = 64 \div$ ___4___

(7) $(7^2 - 5^2) \div 6 = 11 -$ ___7___

$$\begin{array}{r} 49 \\ -25 \\ \hline 24 \end{array}$$

(8) $88 \div (7 + 4) = 96 \div$ ___12___

(9) $121 - (3 + 8) = 11 \times$ ___10___

(10) $55 - 24 \times 2 = 24 -$ ___17___

$$\begin{array}{r} 55 \\ -24 \\ \hline 31 \end{array}$$

Score: .... / 10

Synonyms

You have 6 minutes to complete this test.

You have 10 questions to complete within the time given.

In each question, underline the two words (one from each group) that are most similar in meaning.

EXAMPLE

(<u>funny</u>   annoyed   silent)

(soft   red   <u>entertaining</u>)

---

1 (sky   <u>discuss</u>   compete)

(dive   succeed   <u>debate</u>)

2 (accept   <u>dodge</u>   collect)

(<u>avoid</u>   fairground   money)

3 (lively   <u>idle</u>   hot)

(<u>lazy</u>   sick   tired)

4 (unique   massive   anxious)

(painless   nervous   <u>jagged</u>)

5 (plume   <u>hairy</u>   bird)

(pirate   beard   feather)

6 (quicken   elevate   <u>blossom</u>)

(<u>flower</u>   walk   brush)

7 (nativity   flight   <u>exit</u>)

(ferry   <u>leave</u>   airport)

8 (<u>cry</u>   laugh   scream)

(croak   dare   <u>sob</u>)

9 (stark   <u>enthusiastic</u>   aquatic)

(<u>keen</u>   hopeless   scarlet)

10 (white   raincoat   <u>downpour</u>)

(snow   <u>rain</u>   sleet)

Score: .... / 10

9

Code Sets

You have 6 minutes to complete this test.

You have 9 questions to complete within the time given
(3 sets of codes with 3 questions each).

In each set of questions, three of the four words are given in code. These codes are not in the same order as the words and one code is missing. Use these codes to answer each question and write your answer on the dotted line.

EXAMPLE

PASS	PAST	TEST	BEST
8457	8455	7157	

Find the code for the word **PAST** ....8457.........

BALL	CALF	BOLT	CALL
8355	8152	7354	

(1) Find the code for the word **CALF** ....

(2) Find the word that has the number code **8152** ....

(3) Find the code for the word **CALL** ....

ROSE	HOME	HOSE	ROAM
8753	8713	4725	

(4) Find the code for the word **HOME** ....

(5) Find the word that has the number code **4725** ....

(6) Find the code for the word **ROSE** ....

SEAS	REST	PEAR	REAR
9139	5139	9178	

(7) Find the code for the word **PEAR** ....

(8) Find the word that has the number code **9139** ....

(9) Find the code for the word **SEAS** ....

Score: .... / 9

In each question, underline the two words (one from each group) that will complete the phrase in the best way.

EXAMPLE

Hot is to
(<u>cold</u>   dry   wet)
as **expensive** is to
(hotel   clothes   <u>cheap</u>).

(1) **Peace** is to
(dove   war   charity)
as **fatigue** is to
(hope   anxiety   energy).

(2) **Dog** is to
(cute   puppy   bark)
as **deer** is to
(fawn   field   forest).

(3) **April** is to
(Easter   March   June)
as **December** is to
(November   presents   January).

(4) **Nose** is to
(nostrils   smell   snout)
as **foot** is to
(paw   leg   shoes).

(5) **Future** is to
(week   month   tomorrow)
as **past** is to
(over   yesterday   ancient).

(6) **Rome** is to
(pasta   Italy   gladiator)
as **Athens** is to
(sunshine   Portugal   Greece).

(7) **Mountain** is to
(mountaineer   snow   skiing)
as **sea** is to
(fish   swimming   blue).

(8) **Thermometer** is to
(sun   time   temperature)
as **barometer** is to
(time   pressure   clouds).

(9) **Stale** is to
(smelly   old   fresh)
as **courageous** is to
(knight   cowardly   powerful).

(10) **Ruby** is to
(slipper   costly   red)
as **sapphire** is to
(blue   optimistic   green).

Score: .... / 10

11

Letter Connections

You have 6 minutes to complete this test.

You have 10 questions to complete within the time given.

In each question, write in the letter that fits into both sets of brackets.

The letter should finish the word before the brackets and start the word after the brackets.

EXAMPLE

cal [....l....] ast

bel [....l....] ate   *(The four words are call, last, bell, late.)*

---

(1) kne [............] rong

     sno [............] orry

(2) the [............] awn

     cla [............] olk

(3) magi [............] uddle

     toxi [............] ase

(4) hea [............] ank

     bandi [............] rain

(5) chi [............] lap

     musi [............] rab

(6) mil [............] not

     pin [............] ick

(7) gai [............] eck

     chi [............] one

(8) was [............] int

     slee [............] lug

(9) pan [............] ime

     eas [............] ower

(10) cla [............] ire

      belo [............] in

Score: .... / 10

Hidden Words

In each question, a four-letter word can be found by combining the end of one word with the beginning of the next word.

Underline the two words that contain these letters and write in the new four-letter word.

EXAMPLE

Dinner included mash and peas.   *hand*   (mash **and**)

---

(1) Place an avocado next to the bananas to help them ripen.   ....

(2) Sourav was overcome with emotion.   ....

(3) Did you know Ashley passed all her tests?   ....

(4) I eventually found my bicycle in the attic.   ....

(5) We went to lunch early.   ....

(6) The pineapples should be put in the pantry.   ....

(7) The top athletes did not finish the course.   ....

(8) He could not leave until Lenny was ready.   ....

(9) She looked at the photo adoringly.   ....

(10) The satin yoga jacket is her favourite present.   ....

Score: .... / 10

Code Pairs

You have 6 minutes to complete this test.

You have 10 questions to complete within the time given.

Use the alphabet below to help you with these questions.

ABCDEFGHIJKLMNOPQRSTUVWXYZ

In each question, use the code provided to identify the new word or code.

EXAMPLE

If the code for **ANT** is **APW**, what is the code for **FOG**? .... **FQJ** ....

① If the code for **NECK** is **OFDL**, what is the code for **VASE**? ....

② If the code for **BRAIN** is **IMDHN**, what word is created by the code **ZODSE**? ....

③ If the code for **HAT** is **DEP**, what is the code for **RED**? ....

④ If the code for **KING** is **HKKI**, what word is created by the code **QTXR**? ....

⑤ If the code for **CHIME** is **BGHLD**, what is the code for **KNIFE**? ....

⑥ If the code for **LIGHT** is **HIJHR**, what word is created by the code **ZIDRW**? ....

⑦ If the code for **CLIP** is **ANGR**, what is the code for **SEAT**? ....

⑧ If the code for **LUNCH** is **NRQAJ**, what word is created by the code **DFUBU**? ....

⑨ If the code for **YOUR** is **ZMQM**, what is the code for **WOOD**? ....

⑩ If the code for **LIKE** is **MFPC**, what word is created by the code **SFSE**? ....

Score: .... / 10

Problem Solving

In each question, read the information provided and then write in your answer.

EXAMPLE

Monkey A weighs 23 kg more than Monkey C.

Monkey C is twice the weight of Monkey B who weighs 5 kg.

How much does Monkey A weigh? ....33 kg..........

---

(1) There are 32 cows in a field. One quarter of them are Jersey
cattle and they belong to Farmer Holmes.
The rest are Holstein cows.

**If one sixth of the Holsteins belong to Farmer Jones and
the rest belong to Farmer Boggins, how many cows does
Farmer Boggins have?** ....

(2) It takes 24 builders 8 days to build a conservatory.

**How many days would it take 48 builders to build
an identical conservatory?** ....

(3) David won £36000.
He shared his prize money between 3 people.
Daniel received £6000. Francis got two fifths of the remaining amount
and David got the rest.

What is the total amount David gave away to Daniel and Francis? ....

(4) Mrs Baker has five dogs and she has 42 dog biscuits.
She gives Russell 7 and Buster one seventh of the remaining biscuits.
Rocky gets 14 biscuits.
Mrs Baker then splits the remaining biscuits equally between Buddy
and Charlie.

How many dog biscuits does Buddy get? ....

Questions continue on next page

(5) Davina, Kerry and Amber go to the theatre and sit side by side.
Kerry and Amber don't sit next to each other.
Amber sits on the far left.

Who sits on the far right? ....

(6) Barry is 12 and his grandmother is five times his age.

How old will Barry's grandmother be in 8 years? ....

(7) Dominic's birthday is on 14th November.
Dominic was born on a Tuesday.
Eve was born on 26th November of the same year.

On which day of the week was Eve born? ....

(8) A chicken lays 10 eggs a day.
William uses 3 eggs a day to make an omelette and sells the rest.

After 12 days, how many eggs has he sold? ....

Score: .... / 8

Letter Analogies

Use the alphabet below to help you with these questions.

A B C D E F G H I J K L M N O P Q R S T U V W X Y Z

In each question, write in the letters that will complete the phrase in the best way.

EXAMPLE

BD is to **CF** as **MO** is to .... NQ ....

---

(1) **HI** is to **IH** as **NO** is to ....

(2) **CX** is to **DW** as **GT** is to ....

(3) **ED** is to **FE** as **UT** is to ....

(4) **KN** is to **HK** as **WZ** is to ....

(5) **GX** is to **JX** as **RY** is to ....

(6) **GC** is to **JF** as **MI** is to ....

(7) **KU** is to **KW** as **LV** is to ....

(8) **ZW** is to **WT** as **TQ** is to ....

(9) **JJ** is to **OE** as **RR** is to ....

(10) **BA** is to **AZ** as **KJ** is to ....

Score: .... / 10

Letters for Numbers

You have 6 minutes to complete this test.

You have 10 questions to complete within the time given.

In each question, numbers are shown as letters. Find the answer to the sum and write it in as a letter.

EXAMPLE

A = 5   B = 15   C = 10   D = 4   E = 22
What is the answer to this sum **written as a letter**?   A + B − C = __C__

---

(1) A = 2   B = 30   C = 14   D = 17   E = 5
What is the answer to this sum **written as a letter**?   A + D − C = ...

(2) A = 9   B = 14   C = 2   D = 49   E = 7
What is the answer to this sum **written as a letter**?   A × E − B = ...

(3) A = 10   B = 54   C = 9   D = 6   E = 8
What is the answer to this sum **written as a letter**?   B ÷ C = ...

(4) A = 36   B = 9   C = 27   D = 2   E = 30
What is the answer to this sum **written as a letter**?   D × B × D = ...

(5) A = 4   B = 11   C = 3   D = 6   E = 27
What is the answer to this sum **written as a letter**?   (E + D) ÷ B = ...

(6) A = 18   B = 17   C = 16   D = 11   E = 2
What is the answer to this sum **written as a letter**?   (A + C) ÷ E = ...

(7) A = 14   B = 5   C = 12   D = 8   E = 9
What is the answer to this sum **written as a letter**?   B × B − C − D =..............

(8) A = 9   B = 6   C = 18   D = 10   E = 3
What is the answer to this sum **written as a letter**?   C ÷ B × E = ...

(9) A = 40   B = 5   C = 16   D = 2   E = 20
What is the answer to this sum **written as a letter**?   A ÷ B × D = ...

(10) A = 132   B = 126   C = 12   D = 144   E = 136
What is the answer to this sum **written as a letter**?   C × C − C = ...

Score: .... / 10

Number Sequences

You have 6 minutes to complete this test.

You have 10 questions to complete within the time given.

In each question, write in the number that best completes the sequence.

EXAMPLE

52   54   56   58   60   ....**62**.........

(1)   7   9   11   13   15   ....

(2)   23   20   17   14   11   ....

(3)   17   15   14   12   11   ....

(4)   11   14   12   15   13   ....

(5)   16   21   26   31   36   ....

(6)   3   8   18   23   33   ....

(7)   4000   2000   1000   500   250   ....

(8)   144   121   100   81   64   ....

(9)   16   22   28   34   40   ....

(10)   24   19   23   18   22   ....

Score: .... / 10

Move a Letter

You have 6 minutes to complete this test.

You have 10 questions to complete within the time given.

In each question, one letter can be moved from the first word to the second word to create two new words.

The order of the other letters must not change.

Underline the letter that needs to move, and write in the two new words.

EXAMPLE

raise   pin   rise   pain

---

① ruin   star   ....

② bleach   pan   ....

③ crown   tow   ....

④ train   pun   ....

⑤ brain   each   ....

⑥ front   oar   ....

⑦ know   as   ....

⑧ time   arch   ....

⑨ tramp   sigh   ....

⑩ flood   sash   ....

Score: .... / 10

Word Construction

You have 6 minutes to complete this test.

You have 10 questions to complete within the time given.

In each question, the three words on the second line should go together in the same way as the three words on the first line.

Write in the missing word on the second line.

EXAMPLE

(easy   [self]   flow)

(laps   [........plod........]   does)

---

1   (hero   [roam]   puma)

(vine   [........................]   oats)

2   (pack   [trip]   dirt)

(bull   [........................]   yard)

3   (mole   [malt]   bath)

(clam   [........................]   rota)

4   (ache   [heal]   also)

(bite   [........................]   stop)

5   (loaf   [foam]   arms)

(hair   [........................]   tier)

6   (mast   [past]   rope)

(pole   [........................]   fuss)

7   (envy   [veal]   lamp)

(brow   [........................]   year)

8   (lamb   [bail]   aims)

(golf   [........................]   roam)

9   (sort   [stem]   poem)

(gear   [........................]   stab)

10   (cave   [case]   user)

(heap   [........................]   bell)

Score: .... / 10

Word Combinations

You have 6 minutes to complete this test.

You have 10 questions to complete within the time given.

In each question, combine one word from the first line with one word from the second line to create one new word.

The word from the first line always comes first.

Underline the correct word from each line and write in the new word.

EXAMPLE

(<u>rain</u>   by   open)

(bite   like   <u>bow</u>)   .... **rainbow** ....

---

1 (all   no   ever)

(way   left   body)   ....

2 (camera   photo   snap)

(shut   copy   print)   ....

3 (sea   land   sky)

(rove   barn   scraper)   ....

4 (feat   suit   back)

(table   us   her)   ....

5 (in   foot   down)

(old   load   mobile)   ....

6 (down   up   fore)

(set   fix   pin)   ....

7 (girl   with   for)

(buy   get   power)   ....

8 (house   home   bed)

(draw   keep   hold)   ....

9 (extra   cab   out)

(usual   inn   ordinary)   ....

10 (hay   grass   straw)

(bail   apple   berries)   ....

Score: .... / 10

Double Meanings

You have 6 minutes to complete this test.

You have 10 questions to complete within the time given.

In each question, there are two pairs of words. Write in a new word that goes equally well with both word pairs.

EXAMPLE

(signify   symbolise)

(unkind   nasty)   ....**mean**........

---

1 (enjoy   love)

(similar   resembling)   ....

2 (near   adjacent)

(shut   lock)   ....

3 (observe   look)

(clock   timepiece)   ....

4 (drop   fall)

(basin   bowl)   ....

5 (tiny   little)

(moment   second)   ....

6 (rod   twig)

(fasten   glue)   ....

7 (keep   preserve)

(rescue   aid)   ....

8 (penalty   punishment)

(acceptable   reasonable)   ....

9 (even   uniform)

(apartment   penthouse)   ....

10 (line   column)

(argument   squabble)   ....

Score: .... / 10

23

Related Numbers

You have 6 minutes to complete this test.

You have 10 questions to complete within the time given.

In each question, the three numbers in each group are related in some way.

Write in the number that correctly completes the last group.

EXAMPLE

(2 [7] 9)   (3 [3] 6)   (6 [__8__] 14)

---

① (12 [48] 4)   (10 [60] 6)   (7 [............] 7)

② (50 [44] 6)   (15 [8] 7)   (23 [............] 9)

③ (17 [20] 3)   (5 [19] 14)   (22 [............] 13)

④ (32 [13] 45)   (21 [46] 67)   (23 [............] 86)

⑤ (2 [16] 32)   (4 [22] 88)   (3 [............] 63)

⑥ (11 [26] 7)   (15 [25] 2)   (7 [............] 10)

⑦ (15 [24] 15)   (16 [20] 10)   (14 [............] 8)

⑧ (6 [26] 4)   (5 [32] 6)   (4 [............] 7)

⑨ (7 [25] 2)   (10 [49] 3)   (8 [............] 2)

⑩ (50 [31] 20)   (70 [31] 40)   (80 [............] 20)

Score: .... / 10

Code Sequences

You have 6 minutes to complete this test.

You have 10 questions to complete within the time given.

Use the alphabet below to help you with these questions.

A B C D E F G H I J K L M N O P Q R S T U V W X Y Z

In each question, write in the letters that are next in the sequence.

EXAMPLE

| FB | HB | JC | LC | ND | **PD** |

---

1.   PT   RV   RX   TZ   TB   ....

2.   WS   XQ   YO   ZM   AK   ....

3.   CE   EG   GI   IK   KM   ....

4.   AZ   BX   CV   DT   ER   ....

5.   JU   TU   KU   UU   LU   ....

6.   OO   TN   PP   SM   QQ   ....

7.   TH   UJ   VL   WN   XP   ....

8.   FO   EM   DK   CI   BG   ....

9.   WO   TR   QP   NS   KQ   ....

10.   NN   MO   LP   KQ   JR   ....

Score: .... / 10

Missing Letters

In each question, three letters have been removed from the word in capitals.

These three letters correctly spell a new word without changing their order.

Write in the three missing letters.

EXAMPLE

BCH is a meal usually eaten from late morning to early afternoon. ...._RUN_........

(*The word in capitals is BRUNCH.*)

(1) The old STCASE creaked loudly. ....

(2) I don't UNDERSD what I am supposed to do. ....

(3) TOMAS tend to grow better in sunny countries. ....

(4) Paris is the CAAL of France. ....

(5) The MON swung from branch to branch. ....

(6) The athlete almost COLSED from exhaustion. ....

(7) WRIG stories came naturally to him. ....

(8) Fatima enjoyed BAG cakes in her spare time. ....

(9) The HELITER could be heard overhead. ....

(10) The PAR repeated the same sentence a few times. ....

Score: .... / 10

Antonyms

In each question, underline the two words (one from each group) that are most opposite in meaning.

EXAMPLE

(<u>sad</u>   last   bitter)

(tired   <u>happy</u>   friendly)

---

(1)   (change   target   correct)

(wrong   illegal   remain)

(2)   (enormous   elephant   Chinese)

(mouse   whisper   tiny)

(3)   (always   hardly   rock)

(forever   never   soft)

(4)   (wicked   lift   double)

(good   dig   evil)

(5)   (fire   crash   failure)

(success   accident   warmth)

(6)   (lock   fascinating   stage)

(key   dull   tepid)

(7)   (simple   fresh   inhibited)

(mixed   dangerous   complicated)

(8)   (shady   dark   modern)

(light   suspicious   contemporary)

(9)   (shiny   clean   leadership)

(scheming   dirty   authority)

(10)   (current   forbidden   dumb)

(intelligent   satisfactory   acute)

Score: .... / 10

Related Words

In each question, three of the words are related in some way.

Underline the two words that do not relate to the other three.

EXAMPLE

purple   royal   fruit   orange   grey

(The underlined words are not colours.)

1. spanner   nail   chisel   builder   hammer

2. trousers   cotton   silk   shirt   linen

3. hummingbird   caterpillar   sparrow   dog   penguin

4. soft   scales   feathers   birds   fur

5. beech   shore   birch   sand   oak

6. recliner   comfortable   armchair   sofa   bed

7. calf   cow   cub   bear   tadpole

8. plump   sour   stout   phenomenal   fat

9. dinghy   sailor   yacht   wave   hovercraft

10. boots   metre   shoes   feet   inches

Score: .... / 10

Complete the Sum

In each question, write in the number that correctly completes the sum.

EXAMPLE

$3 + 9 = 6 +$ ....6....

(1) $9 × 6 - 31 = 17 +$ ....

(2) $8 + 25 = 3 ×$ ....

(3) $2 × 12 = 37 -$ ....

(4) $83 - 15 = 3 × 20 +$ ....

(5) $34 + 26 - 15 = 90 ÷$ ....

(6) $8 + 8 = 45 -$ ....

(7) $75 ÷ 5 =$ .... $+ 4$

(8) $8 × 10 = 103 -$ ....

(9) $20 × 3 - 4 = 37 +$ ....

(10) $5 × 5 - 6 = 2 + 7 +$ ....

Score: .... / 10

Synonyms

You have 6 minutes to complete this test.

You have 10 questions to complete within the time given.

In each question, underline the two words (one from each group) that are most similar in meaning.

EXAMPLE

(<u>funny</u>   annoyed   silent)

(soft   red   <u>entertaining</u>)

① (sweet   arid   shabby)

(dry   lazy   furious)

② (shopping   purchase   market)

(farmer   square   buy)

③ (myth   old   fact)

(interpretation   fable   wisdom)

④ (muscle   vast   hill)

(huge   steep   valley)

⑤ (gutter   odour   dog)

(rat   smell   steam)

⑥ (happiness   paradise   heaven)

(agony   joy   hope)

⑦ (mischievous   child   behaviour)

(naughty   strict   faithful)

⑧ (blunt   last   timid)

(sharp   sticky   shy)

⑨ (soak   envy   danger)

(peril   sympathy   bridge)

⑩ (aid   desire   shape)

(signal   ambulance   help)

Score: .... / 10

Code Sets

You have 6 minutes to complete this test.

You have 9 questions to complete within the time given
(3 sets of codes with 3 questions each).

In each set of questions, three of the four words are given in code. These codes are not in the same order as the words and one code is missing. Use these codes to answer each question and write your answer on the dotted line.

EXAMPLE

PASS	PAST	TEST	BEST
8457	8455	7157	

Find the code for the word **PAST** ....8457.........

FISH	WIFE	CHEF	WISH
5893	6278	3278	

(1) Find the code for the word **CHEF** ....

(2) Find the word that has the number code **6278** ....

(3) Find the code for the word **WIFE** ....

NEST	STAR	BARN	BARS
7432	7438	8529	

(4) Find the code for the word **BARN** ....

(5) Find the word that has the number code **8529** ....

(6) Find the code for the word **STAR** ....

FILM	LIME	MILL	MILE
8344	4387	6348	

(7) Find the code for the word **MILL** ....

(8) Find the word that has the number code **4387** ....

(9) Find the code for the word **MILE** ....

Score: .... / 9

Test	Word Analogies
28	You have 6 minutes to complete this test. You have 10 questions to complete within the time given.

In each question, underline the two words (one from each group) that will complete the phrase in the best way.

EXAMPLE

Hot is to
(<u>cold</u>   dry   wet)
as **expensive** is to
(hotel   clothes   <u>cheap</u>).

1. **Miserable** is to
   (cheerful   downcast   glorious)
   as **important** is to
   (essential   transparent   serious).

2. **Cook** is to
   (bread   delicious   kitchen)
   as **teacher** is to
   (students   classroom   maths).

3. **Throw** is to
   (ball   hurl   catch)
   as **change** is to
   (alter   money   spring).

4. **Desert** is to
   (sweet   sand   hot)
   as **rainforest** is to
   (monkey   Amazon   trees).

5. **Cow** is to
   (hide   milk   field)
   as **snake** is to
   (scary   slither   scales).

6. **Asia** is to
   (China   continent   noodles)
   as **Madrid** is to
   (Spanish   city   hamlet).

7. **Orange** is to
   (yellow   juicy   fruit)
   as **chicken** is to
   (meat   hen   barbecue).

8. **Lie** is to
   (false   down   lay)
   as **sell** is to
   (sold   shopkeeper   customer).

9. **History** is to
   (historical   subject   ancient)
   as **accident** is to
   (slippery   crash   accidental).

10. **Extraordinary** is to
    (normal   miraculous   sheep)
    as **uncomfortable** is to
    (sofa   heat   unbearable).

Score: .... / 10

Letter Connections

In each question, write in the letter that fits into both sets of brackets.

The letter should finish the word before the brackets and start the word after the brackets.

EXAMPLE

cal [....l....] ast

bel [....l....] ate   *(The four words are call, last, bell, late.)*

---

(1)   hos [.............] our

sho [.............] arget

(2)   lea [.............] old

wol [.............] ist

(3)   muc [.............] eel

bot [.............] old

(4)   nea [.............] ose

sca [.............] eason

(5)   sin [.............] ate

mu [.............] ang

(6)   pea [.............] ice

roa [.............] ace

(7)   ti [.............] est

sati [.............] ewt

(8)   pro [.............] ouse

far [.............] ale

(9)   was [.............] all

ranc [.............] eat

(10) chil [.............] ime

ban [.............] oor

Score: .... / 10

Test	# Hidden Words
30	You have 6 minutes to complete this test.
	You have 10 questions to complete within the time given.

In each question, a four-letter word can be found by combining the end of one word with the beginning of the next word.

Underline the two words that contain these letters and write in the new four-letter word.

EXAMPLE

Dinner included <u>mash and</u> peas.   ....**hand**.........   (*mash **and***)

(**1**) Eventually, Laura showed us where to go.   ....

(**2**) The parrot tried to mimic every visitor.   ....

(**3**) Small cubs are usually within earshot of their mothers.   ....

(**4**) Maybe escaping isn't as easy as it looks.   ....

(**5**) Nobody peels potatoes as quickly as he does.   ....

(**6**) The vicar decided to go for a walk.   ....

(**7**) After one month, another card will be sent to you.   ....

(**8**) Peter threw inks over the sheet to create his artwork.   ....

(**9**) After the picnic, Nancy went for a walk.   ....

(**10**) Dermot allowed his nephews to take some sweets.   ....

Score: .... / 10

Code Pairs

Use the alphabet below to help you with these questions.

A B C D E F G H I J K L M N O P Q R S T U V W X Y Z

In each question, use the code provided to identify the new word or code.

EXAMPLE

If the code for **ANT** is **APW**, what is the code for **FOG**? ....FQJ.............

1. If the code for **CALM** is **EDMQ**, what word is created by the code **DRBX**? ....

2. If the code for **PLAY** is **UQFD**, what is the code for **TAXI**? ....

3. If the code for **CHEESE** is **HHZEXE**, what is the code for **PUZZLE**? ....

4. If the code for **COOK** is **FNRJ**, what word is created by the code **VDOK**? ....

5. If the code for **ANGER** is **GSKHT**, what is the code for **DREAM**? ....

6. If the code for **SCORE** is **PDLSB**, what is the code for **DENIM**? ....

7. If the code for **BOOK** is **KOOC**, what word is created by the code **TSAD**? ....

8. If the code for **MILK** is **OLNN**, what word is created by the code **JDVH**? ....

9. If the code for **DUMP** is **IOPR**, what is the code for **PILE**? ....

10. If the code for **GALE** is **FZJC**, what word is created by the code **QZGL**? ....

Score: .... / 10

Problem Solving

You have 6 minutes to complete this test.

You have 8 questions to complete within the time given.

In each question, read the information provided and then write in your answer.

EXAMPLE

Monkey A weighs 23 kg more than Monkey C.

Monkey C is twice the weight of Monkey B who weighs 5 kg.

How much does Monkey A weigh?

.............*33 kg*.............

---

(1) Allan has £5.10.

He buys a pot of jam for £2.40.

If chocolate bars cost 45p each, how many chocolate bars can Allan buy with the remaining coins?

....

(2) Vivian is three years younger than Rachel.

Rachel is half the age of Mandy.

If Mandy is 22, how old is Vivian?

....

(3) Phillip spent $\frac{2}{4}$ of his money on sweets and $\frac{1}{3}$ of his money on books.

If he has £4.50 left over, how much money did he have at the start?

....

(4) The school bus stops 15 times.

It takes 3 minutes between each stop.

If the bus leaves at 3.27 pm, what time will it arrive at the last stop?

....

(5) Francis's watch is 10 minutes fast.

The classroom clock is running 15 minutes slow and says 1.30 pm.

What time will Francis's watch show? ....

(6) Mrs Green and Mrs Williams leave the meeting at the same time.

Mrs Williams leaves at 4 pm and arrives home 45 minutes later.

Mrs Green's journey takes four times as long as Mrs Williams' journey.

What time will Mrs Green arrive home? ....

(7) Three dogs weigh 54 kg in total.

Dog A weighs 22 kg. Dog B weighs 15 kg.

How much more does Dog A weigh than Dog C? ....

(8) Sue is three times older than her brother, Alexander.

**If Alexander will be 10 in 2 years,
how old is Sue now?** ....

Score: .... / 8

Letter Analogies

Use the alphabet below to help you with these questions.

ABCDEFGHIJKLMNOPQRSTUVWXYZ

In each question, write in the letters that will complete the phrase in the best way.

EXAMPLE

BD is to **CF** as **MO** is to .... NQ ....

---

(1) **HF** is to **LJ** as **BZ** is to ....

(2) **ID** is to **EM** as **UP** is to ....

(3) **DI** is to **HM** as **MR** is to ....

(4) **DH** is to **JC** as **WA** is to ....

(5) **PL** is to **TE** as **GC** is to ....

(6) **HL** is to **OS** as **EI** is to ....

(7) **XC** is to **SK** as **LQ** is to ....

(8) **GE** is to **IG** as **OM** is to ....

(9) **JK** is to **LL** as **RS** is to ....

(10) **ZW** is to **BP** as **PM** is to ....

Score: .... / 10

Letters for Numbers

You have 6 minutes to complete this test.

You have 10 questions to complete within the time given.

In each question, numbers are shown as letters. Find the answer to the sum and write it in as a letter.

EXAMPLE

A = 5   B = 15   C = 10   D = 4   E = 22
What is the answer to this sum **written as a letter**?   A + B – C = ___C___

1   A = 2   B = 6   C = 3   D = 8   E = 10
What is the answer to this sum **written as a letter**?   A × D – B = ...

2   A = 6   B = 5   C = 7   D = 10   E = 20
What is the answer to this sum **written as a letter**?   E – D – B = ...

3   A = 7   B = 6   C = 4   D = 9   E = 5
What is the answer to this sum **written as a letter**?   D + C – A = ...

4   A = 15   B = 4   C = 9   D = 7   E = 2
What is the answer to this sum **written as a letter**?   A – B × E = ...

5   A = 4   B = 8   C = 10   D = 6   E = 20
What is the answer to this sum **written as a letter**?   E – A – D = ...

6   A = 9   B = 12   C = 6   D = 3   E = 1
What is the answer to this sum **written as a letter**?   D × E + C = ...

7   A = 12   B = 3   C = 8   D = 5   E = 6
What is the answer to this sum **written as a letter**?   B × C – A = ...

8   A = 10   B = 12   C = 20   D = 5   E = 2
What is the answer to this sum **written as a letter**?   C ÷ A × D + A =................

9   A = 7   B = 4   C = 6   D = 3   E = 15
What is the answer to this sum **written as a letter**?   A × D – C = ...

10   A = 3   B = 7   C = 8   D = 5   E = 2
What is the answer to this sum **written as a letter**?   E + C – B = ...

Score: .... / 10

In each question, write in the number that best completes the sequence.

EXAMPLE

52   54   56   58   60   .... **62** ....

(1)   50   35   20   5   −10   ....

(2)   37   99   31   103   25   ....

(3)   4   8   7   11   10   ....

(4)   90   72   100   63   110   ....

(5)   14   8   28   16   42   ....

(6)   13   17   21   25   29   ....

(7)   32   29   26   23   20   ....

(8)   19   31   22   28   25   ....

(9)   17   29   41   53   65   ....

(10)   6   9   11   14   16   ....

Score: .... / 10

Move a Letter

In each question, one letter can be moved from the first word to the second word to create two new words.

The order of the other letters must not change.

Underline the letter that needs to move, and write in the two new words.

EXAMPLE

r<u>a</u>ise   pin   rise   pain

---

1   noise   deal   ....

2   flower   scar   ....

3   clock   row   ....

4   brake   owl   ....

5   musty   bus   ....

6   curse   tone   ....

7   grown   pay   ....

8   hour   tick   ....

9   heard   very   ....

10 soap   mat   ....

Score: .... / 10

Word Construction

You have 6 minutes to complete this test.

You have 10 questions to complete within the time given.

In each question, the three words on the second line should go together in the same way as the three words on the first line.

Write in the missing word on the second line.

EXAMPLE

(easy   [self]   flow)

(laps   [....... _plod_ ....]   does)

---

1   (step   [dips]   find)

(darn   [.........................]   taps)

2   (pore   [torn]   newt)

(nine   [.........................]   gawk)

3   (very   [grey]   game)

(glue   [.........................]   hang)

4   (joke   [pork]   reap)

(pity   [.........................]   scam)

5   (pond   [lend]   left)

(walk   [.........................]   four)

6   (task   [cost]   echo)

(sane   [.........................]   idle)

7   (fuse   [fist]   twig)

(bone   [.........................]   dean)

8   (eels   [tile]   trim)

(real   [.........................]   blob)

9   (gong   [amen]   same)

(boys   [.........................]   farm)

10   (hook   [knot]   unit)

(want   [.........................]   pure)

Score: .... / 10

Word Combinations

You have 6 minutes to complete this test.

You have 10 questions to complete within the time given.

In each question, combine one word from the first line with one word from the second line to create one new word.

The word from the first line always comes first.

Underline the correct word from each line and write in the new word.

EXAMPLE

(<u>rain</u>   by   open)

(bite   like   <u>bow</u>)   ....**rainbow**..........

---

1 (lake   sea   marine)

(ship   back   gull)   ....

2 (table   data   foot)

(base   site   wore)   ....

3 (palm   nail   hand)

(tree   some   clip)   ....

4 (straw   port   for)

(rug   mat   mop)   ....

5 (life   fate   be)

(all   ill   time)   ....

6 (is   brake   on)

(time   fast   land)   ....

7 (under   side   hair)

(growth   ware   pan)   ....

8 (lake   dam   law)

(sill   old   age)   ....

9 (fruit   meat   butter)

(platter   dish   cup)   ....

10 (back   toe   ear)

(wing   drum   spot)   ....

Score: .... / 10

Double Meanings

In each question, there are two pairs of words. Write in a new word that goes equally well with both word pairs.

EXAMPLE

(signify   symbolise)

(unkind   nasty)   ....**mean**........

1. (leap   jump)

   (summer   autumn)   ....

2. (lamp   illumination)

   (bright   sunny)   ....

3. (recline   sprawl)

   (falsehood   deceit)   ....

4. (howl   yelp)

   (covering   skin)   ....

5. (split   rip)

   (drop   bead)   ....

6. (correspond   equal)

   (contest   game)   ....

7. (conceal   bury)

   (pelt   skin)   ....

8. (slip   stumble)

   (excursion   journey)   ....

9. (nod   curtsy)

   (knot   loop)   ....

10. (considerate   loving)

    (sort   type)   ....

Score: .... / 10

Related Numbers

You have 6 minutes to complete this test.

You have 10 questions to complete within the time given.

In each question, the three numbers in each group are related in some way.

Write in the number that correctly completes the last group.

EXAMPLE

(2   [7]   9)   (3   [3]   6)   (6   [__8__]   14)

1. (132   [12]   11)   (75   [15]   5)   (60   [............]   4)

2. (20   [46]   3)   (16   [42]   5)   (14   [............]   20)

3. (47   [16]   15)   (18   [5]   8)   (45   [............]   33)

4. (40   [70]   20)   (4   [25]   11)   (24   [............]   31)

5. (29   [50]   21)   (33   [45]   12)   (36   [............]   19)

6. (4   [22]   9)   (9   [37]   14)   (2   [............]   19)

7. (67   [49]   18)   (99   [73]   26)   (82   [............]   33)

8. (5   [90]   9)   (8   [96]   6)   (9   [............]   4)

9. (12   [26]   10)   (10   [29]   1)   (25   [............]   2)

10. (33   [13]   47)   (20   [1]   22)   (29   [............]   45)

Score: .... / 10

You have 6 minutes to complete this test.

You have 10 questions to complete within the time given.

Use the alphabet below to help you with these questions.

A B C D E F G H I J K L M N O P Q R S T U V W X Y Z

In each question, write in the letters that are next in the sequence.

EXAMPLE

FB   HB   JC   LC   ND   ....**PD**........

① WO   ZL   CP   FM   IQ   ....

② OJ   XK   NL   VM   MN   ....

③ TY   WW   TU   VS   TQ   ....

④ VE   UN   TE   SL   RE   ....

⑤ CO   CO   BN   DN   AM   ....

⑥ PD   SB   PZ   SX   PV   ....

⑦ CJ   DK   FJ   GL   IJ   ....

⑧ PO   NP   LQ   JR   HS   ....

⑨ II   KH   KG   MF   ME   ....

⑩ KR   LQ   MP   NO   ON   ....

Score: .... / 10

Missing Letters

You have 6 minutes to complete this test.

You have 10 questions to complete within the time given.

In each question, three letters have been removed from the word in capitals.

These three letters correctly spell a new word without changing their order.

Write in the three missing letters.

EXAMPLE

BCH is a meal usually eaten from late morning to early afternoon. .... *RUN* ....

(*The word in capitals is BRUNCH.*)

(1) Every cyclist should wear a HET. ....

(2) HOMEE strawberry jam is delicious. ....

(3) The best salad dressing is with honey and MUSD. ....

(4) The volunteers cleared the BISH from the beach. ....

(5) The world's largest VOLO is in Hawaii. ....

(6) Victoria will turn NIY next month. ....

(7) Add the pasta to BING water. ....

(8) What do you want to eat for DER? ....

(9) The DROBE was full of old clothes and shoes. ....

(10) That SUPERMET is closed on Sundays. ....

Score: .... / 10

In each question, underline the two words (one from each group) that are most opposite in meaning.

EXAMPLE

(<u>sad</u>   last   bitter)

(tired   <u>happy</u>   friendly)

① (warning   jackpot   reward)
   (punish   caution   gratitude)

② (capture   steady   running)
   (temporary   devout   release)

③ (second   first   trunk)
   (last   minute   hand)

④ (deny   aggressive   hesitant)
   (firm   forceful   confirm)

⑤ (treble   cut   shrink)
   (base   grow   total)

⑥ (trust   faithful   certain)
   (doubtful   confident   gullible)

⑦ (underage   minimum   minor)
   (ancient   old   maximum)

⑧ (ready   snappy   rapid)
   (unqualified   slow   cool)

⑨ (full   precise   blunt)
   (sharp   loose   bumpy)

⑩ (trim   neat   sophisticated)
   (smart   knotted   untidy)

Score: .... / 10

48

Related Words

In each question, three of the words are related in some way.

Underline the two words that do not relate to the other three.

EXAMPLE

purple   <u>royal</u>   <u>fruit</u>   orange   grey

(*The underlined words are not colours.*)

1. boater   liner   trilby   sea   beret

2. plaice   place   salmon   meeting   sole

3. fix   mend   spot   ease   repair

4. attic   house   cellar   bed   cloakroom

5. curious   delighted   bleak   interested   inquisitive

6. trip   fall   voyage   slippery   expedition

7. tune   guitar   melody   song   violin

8. backpack   satchel   school   blackboard   suitcase

9. paintbrush   sketch   artist   drawing   illustration

10. architect   apprentice   lawyer   student   dentist

Score: .... / 10

Complete the Sum

In each question, write in the number that correctly completes the sum.

EXAMPLE

$3 + 9 = 6 +$ ....**6**....

① $18 \div 9 = 16 \div$ ....

② $10 \times 11 = 104 +$ ....

③ $86 - 26 = 5 \times$ ....

④ $57 - 3 = 6 \times$ ....

⑤ $131 - 65 =$ .... $\times 11$

⑥ $300 - 190 = 10 +$ ....

⑦ $17 - 6 =$ .... $\div 2$

⑧ $40 \div 8 = 23 -$ ....

⑨ $6 + 5 + 8 = 25 -$ ....

⑩ $50 - (25 + 15) = 9 +$ ....

Score: .... / 10

In each question, underline the two words (one from each group) that are most similar in meaning.

EXAMPLE

(<u>funny</u>   annoyed   silent)

(soft   red   <u>entertaining</u>)

---

1 (buckle   finish   vacant)

(stare   empty   bonnet)

2 (pen   paper   answer)

(write   response   question)

3 (perfume   nose   lovely)

(stench   fragrance   spray)

4 (limb   white   straw)

(pail   brook   leg)

5 (concern   iron   cabbage)

(worry   light   bottle)

6 (comprehend   repent   rehearse)

(perform   understand   riot)

7 (ritual   right   leader)

(habit   patriot   pauper)

8 (computer   pottery   river)

(stream   mouse   island)

9 (plant   affection   show)

(fondness   smile   rose)

10 (fork   soil   spade)

(stone   spoon   shovel)

Score: .... / 10

Code Sets

You have 6 minutes to complete this test.

You have 9 questions to complete within the time given
(3 sets of codes with 3 questions each).

In each set of questions, three of the four words are given in code. These codes are not in the same order as the words and one code is missing. Use these codes to answer each question and write your answer on the dotted line.

EXAMPLE

PASS	PAST	TEST	BEST
8457	8455	7157	

Find the code for the word **PAST**   **8457**

PEST	TRIP	STEM	STEP
3765	7281	3761	

(1) Find the code for the word **STEP**   ....

(2) Find the word that has the number code **7281**   ....

(3) Find the code for the word **PEST**   ....

TOMB	BONE	NONE	KNOT
9792	4975	5786	

(4) Find the code for the word **NONE**   ....

(5) Find the word that has the number code **4975**   ....

(6) Find the code for the word **BONE**   ....

HOOD	DOOM	MOOD	MOTH
5663	2663	5612	

(7) Find the code for the word **HOOD**   ....

(8) Find the word that has the number code **5612**   ....

(9) Find the code for the word **DOOM**   ....

Score: .... / 9

Word Analogies

In each question, underline the two words (one from each group) that will complete the phrase in the best way.

EXAMPLE

Hot is to
(cold   dry   wet)
as **expensive** is to
(hotel   clothes   cheap).

---

(1) **Bear** is to
(grizzly   cub   endure)
as **permit** is to
(allow   parking   form).

(2) **Remedy** is to
(cold   cure   renovate)
as **coherent** is to
(muddled   expensive   logical).

(3) **Ruler** is to
(leader   king   length)
as **compass** is to
(expedition   direction   height).

(4) **Terminate** is to
(end   terminator   depart)
as **assist** is to
(complete   dawdle   help).

(5) **Probable** is to
(conceivable   unavoidable   unlikely)
as **late** is to
(deceptive   ordinary   punctual).

(6) **Vessel** is to
(blood   liquid   boat)
as **attire** is to
(clothes   bird   car).

(7) **Pint** is to
(milk   gallon   beer)
as **inch** is to
(slow   toe   yard).

(8) **House** is to
(build   home   bricks)
as **pan** is to
(metal   cook   boil).

(9) **Tedious** is to
(boring   gloomy   interesting)
as **light** is to
(warmth   sun   illumination).

(10) **Drink** is to
(glass   thirsty   water)
as **breath** is to
(air   inhale   mouth).

Score: .... / 10

Letter Connections

In each question, write in the letter that fits into both sets of brackets.

The letter should finish the word before the brackets and start the word after the brackets.

EXAMPLE

cal [......l......] ast

bel [......l......] ate   *(The four words are call, last, bell, late.)*

(**1**) mas [...............] iss

roc [...............] eep

(**2**) ru [...............] ift

wrin [...............] rain

(**3**) foo [...............] ust

moo [...............] ear

(**4**) mani [...............] rop

publi [...............] ows

(**5**) inhal [...............] njoy

argu [...............] ggs

(**6**) suc [...............] ound

peac [...............] and

(**7**) due [...............] ask

lif [...............] ar

(**8**) fou [...............] aft

hai [...............] est

(**9**) sla [...............] oor

ite [...............] ail

(**10**) lam [...............] old

sta [...............] rain

Score: .... / 10

Hidden Words

You have 6 minutes to complete this test.

You have 10 questions to complete within the time given.

In each question, a four-letter word can be found by combining the end of one word with the beginning of the next word.

Underline the two words that contain these letters and write in the new four-letter word.

EXAMPLE

Dinner included <u>mash and</u> peas. ....**hand**........ (ma**sh and**)

---

(1) Meghan and Allan did not tidy their rooms. ....

(2) The female panda tenderly clutched her cub. ....

(3) If you leave it in the fridge, it becomes soggy. ....

(4) The guests asked for a bathrobe and some coffee. ....

(5) It is a fantastic, old game that has been around for centuries. ....

(6) Which instrument do you play? ....

(7) The teacher eventually finished marking. ....

(8) Fadwa spent her holidays in Greece. ....

(9) Granny watched them eating her casserole. ....

(10) After a day in the sun, the sidecar temperature was unbearable. ....

Score: .... / 10

Code Pairs

You have 6 minutes to complete this test.

You have 10 questions to complete within the time given.

Use the alphabet below to help you with these questions.

ABCDEFGHIJKLMNOPQRSTUVWXYZ

In each question, use the code provided to identify the new word or code.

EXAMPLE

If the code for **ANT** is **APW**, what is the code for **FOG**? .... FQJ ....

(1) If the code for **JAZZ** is **KXBX**, what word is created by the code **MXEC**? ....

(2) If the code for **FAN** is **NFQ**, what word is created by the code **WQG**? ....

(3) If the code for **GLUE** is **JNRC**, what is the code for **HOPE**? ....

(4) If the code for **PINT** is **SKRV**, what is the code for **WASP**? ....

(5) If the code for **SCRUB** is **SHRPB**, what is the word created
by the code **TMRZE**? ....

(6) If the code for **ZEBRA** is **XBXMU**, what is the code for **HORSE**? ....

(7) If the code for **HIVE** is **KJYF**, what word is created by the code **GJFF**? ....

(8) If the code for **CHAP** is **DIBQ**, what is the code for **HAZE**? ....

(9) If the code for **VEX** is **LUN**, what word is created by the code **CQD**? ....

(10) If the code for **WIDOW** is **ROAHV**, what is the code for **SHOES**? ....

Score: .... / 10

In each question, read the information provided and then write in your answer.

EXAMPLE

Monkey A weighs 23 kg more than Monkey C.

Monkey C is twice the weight of Monkey B who weighs 5 kg.

How much does Monkey A weigh? .... *33 kg* ....

(1) It takes Richard 16 minutes to drive from his house to the train station and 4 minutes to buy his ticket.

If his train leaves at 7.52 am and arrives in Southampton at 8.57 am, what is Richard's total journey time between leaving his house and arriving in Southampton? ....

(2) Louise is three times as old as Katie.
In 7 years' time, Louise will be 19.

How old will Katie be in 2 years? ....

(3) If four days after tomorrow is Thursday,
which day was yesterday? ....

(4) My clock is 12 minutes slow.
Simon's watch is 15 minutes fast and says 4.28 pm.

What time does my clock say? ....

(5) 8 pandas eat 36 bananas in 4 days.

How many pandas will eat 72 bananas in 4 days? ....

Questions continue on next page

(6) Nick, Max and Joanna drive to the cinema.

Max leaves at 5.30 pm and Joanne leaves at 8 pm. Joanne's journey is 30 minutes.

If Nick leaves 45 minutes after Max and they all arrive at the same time, how long is Nick's journey?

....

(7) Three wolves A, B and C weigh a total of 76 kg.

Wolf A weighs 31 kg and Wolf B weighs 18 kg.

How much more does Wolf C weigh than Wolf B?

....

(8) It usually takes me 25 minutes to get to school.

I usually arrive at school at 8 am.

However, today there is a road closure and I have to leave 17 minutes earlier to make sure I arrive on time.

What time do I have to leave by?

....

Score: .... / 8

Letter Analogies

You have 6 minutes to complete this test.

You have 10 questions to complete within the time given.

Use the alphabet below to help you with these questions.

A B C D E F G H I J K L M N O P Q R S T U V W X Y Z

In each question, write in the letters that will complete the phrase in the best way.

EXAMPLE

BD is to **CF** as **MO** is to ....NQ........

---

1. **BC** is to **KL** as **FG** is to ....

2. **BG** is to **EA** as **NS** is to ....

3. **PR** is to **QS** as **JL** is to ....

4. **LP** is to **JS** as **TX** is to ....

5. **HM** is to **JO** as **OT** is to ....

6. **FB** is to **OK** as **JF** is to ....

7. **NI** is to **KF** as **WR** is to ....

8. **GL** is to **FN** as **PT** is to ....

9. **VW** is to **PQ** as **MN** is to ....

10. **BF** is to **GK** as **OS** is to ....

Score: .... / 10

Test	**Letters for Numbers**
54	You have 6 minutes to complete this test.
	You have 10 questions to complete within the time given.

In each question, numbers are shown as letters. Find the answer to the sum and write it in as a letter.

EXAMPLE

A = 5   B = 15   C = 10   D = 4   E = 22
What is the answer to this sum **written as a letter**?   A + B − C = __C__

---

(1) A = 11   B = 17   C = 5   D = 8   E = 45
What is the answer to this sum **written as a letter**?   E ÷ C + D = ...

(2) A = 9   B = 10   C = 0   D = 5   E = 2
What is the answer to this sum **written as a letter**?   D × E × C = ...

(3) A = 8   B = 12   C = 19   D = 3   E = 7
What is the answer to this sum **written as a letter**?   (B + C − E) ÷ A = ...

(4) A = 2   B = 0   C = 15   D = 9   E = 18
What is the answer to this sum **written as a letter**?   D × A − D = ...

(5) A = 9   B = 48   C = 8   D = 24   E = 7
What is the answer to this sum **written as a letter**?   (B + D) ÷ C = ...

(6) A = 6   B = 27   C = 9   D = 0   E = 21
What is the answer to this sum **written as a letter**?   E + A − B = ...

(7) A = 90   B = 80   C = 2   D = 70   E = 50
What is the answer to this sum **written as a letter**?   (A − E) × C = ...

(8) A = 44   B = 12   C = 48   D = 8   E = 46
What is the answer to this sum **written as a letter**?   B × D − C = ...

(9) A = 86   B = 24   C = 51   D = 98   E = 11
What is the answer to this sum **written as a letter**?   A − (B + C) = ...

(10) A = 16   B = 3   C = 14   D = 5   E = 13
What is the answer to this sum **written as a letter**?   B × D + C − A = ...

Score: .... / 10

Number Sequences

You have 6 minutes to complete this test.

You have 10 questions to complete within the time given.

In each question, write in the number that best completes the sequence.

EXAMPLE

52   54   56   58   60   .... **62** ....

(1)   49   36   25   16   9   ....

(2)   1   3   −1   1   −3   ....

(3)   2   3   1   2   0   ....

(4)   75   60   45   30   15   ....

(5)   101   202   303   404   505   ....

(6)   103   106   111   118   127   ....

(7)   2   4   8   16   32   ....

(8)   4   2   5   3   6   ....

(9)   63   93   123   153   183   ....

(10)   97   80   63   46   29   ....

Score: .... / 10

Move a Letter

You have 6 minutes to complete this test.

You have 10 questions to complete within the time given.

In each question, one letter can be moved from the first word to the second word to create two new words.

The order of the other letters must not change.

Underline the letter that needs to move, and write in the two new words.

EXAMPLE

raise   pin   .... rise .... pain ....

(1) grub   thin   ....

(2) cheap   sore   ....

(3) cute   read   ....

(4) cloud   bath   ....

(5) paint   best   ....

(6) weight   seal   ....

(7) bland   lame   ....

(8) first   bass   ....

(9) fund   rain   ....

(10) knit   brow   ....

Score: .... / 10

Word Construction

You have 6 minutes to complete this test.

You have 10 questions to complete within the time given.

In each question, the three words on the second line should go together in the same way as the three words on the first line.

Write in the missing word on the second line.

EXAMPLE

(easy   [self]   flow)

(laps   [*plod*]   does)

---

1 (moss   [stem]   teak)

(moat   [................]   rant)

2 (idea   [hide]   heat)

(oval   [................]   meat)

3 (rage   [grew]   west)

(nose   [................]   worm)

4 (lead   [gold]   ogre)

(cake   [................]   ales)

5 (reed   [dark]   rank)

(chef   [................]   pace)

6 (gale   [eggs]   slang)

(idol   [................]   eaten)

7 (duck   [acid]   axis)

(yelp   [................]   peat)

8 (soul   [soup]   past)

(calf   [................]   luck)

9 (hats   [shoe]   pose)

(lick   [................]   tube)

10 (land   [mold]   most)

(need   [................]   wait)

Score: .... / 10

Word Combinations

In each question, combine one word from the first line with one word from the second line to create one new word.

The word from the first line always comes first.

Underline the correct word from each line and write in the new word.

EXAMPLE

(<u>rain</u>   by   open)

(bite   like   <u>bow</u>)   .... rainbow ....

---

1 (pull   rest   pop)

(up   over   in)   ....

2 (counter   chest   one)

(board   act   robe)   ....

3 (throw   hit   pass)

(up   parcel   word)   ....

4 (eat   jump   friend)

(in   ship   worthy)   ....

5 (rat   cow   bee)

(let   him   her)   ....

6 (be   for   ever)

(rear   back   hind)   ....

7 (out   in   wall)

(site   shop   stall)   ....

8 (water   rain   sea)

(jacket   son   boy)   ....

9 (ate   whole   well)

(some   able   cam)   ....

10 (bright   dark   sun)

(fire   light   torch)   ....

Score: .... / 10

Double Meanings

You have 6 minutes to complete this test.

You have 10 questions to complete within the time given.

In each question, there are two pairs of words. Write in a new word that goes equally well with both word pairs.

EXAMPLE

(signify   symbolise)

(unkind   nasty) ....**mean**............

---

1 (enclosure   hutch)

(marker   biro) ....

2 (complimentary   costless)

(release   liberate) ....

3 (only   merely)

(lawful   fair) ....

4 (guide   direct)

(metal   steel) ....

5 (decease   perish)

(cube   counter) ....

6 (current   existing)

(gift   offering) ....

7 (coins   money)

(transform   alter) ....

8 (symbol   mark)

(autograph   subscribe) ....

9 (curtain   shroud)

(conceal   hide) ....

10 (regulation   law)

(govern   reign) ....

Score: .... / 10

Related Numbers

You have 6 minutes to complete this test.

You have 10 questions to complete within the time given.

In each question, the three numbers in each group are related in some way.

Write in the number that correctly completes the last group.

EXAMPLE

(2   [7]   9)   (3   [3]   6)   (6   [__8__]   14)

①   (77   [13]   7)   (48   [6]   12)   (96   [............]   8)

②   (16   [26]   6)   (25   [48]   2)   (35   [............]   6)

③   (5   [42]   7)   (5   [36]   6)   (10   [............]   11)

④   (8   [33]   4)   (9   [55]   6)   (4   [............]   4)

⑤   (25   [1]   50)   (3   [11]   36)   (8   [............]   96)

⑥   (30   [13]   90)   (8   [17]   56)   (10   [............]   50)

⑦   (15   [9]   3)   (26   [13]   10)   (38   [............]   19)

⑧   (12   [108]   9)   (7   [63]   9)   (6   [............]   8)

⑨   (10   [106]   6)   (8   [67]   3)   (9   [............]   5)

⑩   (47   [43]   4)   (94   [89]   5)   (81   [............]   6)

Score: .... / 10

Answers

Test 1 Code Sequences

Q1 **TT** (1st letter: +2, 2nd letter: +2)
Q2 **LC** (1st letter: +1, 2nd letter: +0, +1, +0, +1, +0)
Q3 **RL** (1st letter: +1, 2nd letter: −2)
Q4 **CL** (1st letter: −1, 2nd letter: +2)
Q5 **UF** (1st letter: +1, 2nd letter: +0, +2, +0, +2, +0)
Q6 **FG** (1st letter: +1, 2nd letter: +1)
Q7 **TN** (1st letter: +2, 2nd letter: +1)
Q8 **HX** (1st letter: +1, 2nd letter: +0, −1, +0, −1, +0)
Q9 **PL** (1st letter: +1, +1, +1, −1, −1, 2nd letter: +2)
Q10 **VI** (1st letter: −4, 2nd letter: +3)

Test 2 Missing Letters

Q1 **PUT** (the word in capitals is COMPUTER)
Q2 **ILL** (the word in capitals is GORILLAS)
Q3 **ICE** (the word in capitals is PRACTICE)
Q4 **TEA** (the word in capitals is TEACHER)
Q5 **ASK** (the word in capitals is BASKET)
Q6 **LAY** (the word in capitals is PLAYED)
Q7 **PIN** (the word in capitals is SHOPPING)
Q8 **OUR** (the word in capitals is FLOUR)
Q9 **LIP** (the word in capitals is SLIPPERY)
Q10 **OAT** (the word in capitals is THROAT)

Test 3 Antonyms

Q1 innocent, guilty
Q2 nervous, relaxed
Q3 wide, narrow
Q4 delicious, tasteless
Q5 lucky, unfortunate
Q6 deliberate, unintentional
Q7 permanent, temporary
Q8 tomorrow, yesterday
Q9 strange, ordinary
Q10 energetic, lethargic

Test 4 Related Words

Q1 keys, pitch (all the others are musical instruments)

Q2 bucket, soil (all the others are gardening tools)
Q3 wrist, jewellery (all the others are types of jewellery)
Q4 field, garden (all the others are types of flowers)
Q5 wheel, transport (all the others are types of transport)
Q6 princess, royal (all the others are places of residence)
Q7 over, under (all the others are words related to time)
Q8 skin, freckles (all the others are organs inside the body)
Q9 square, triangle (all the others are three-dimensional shapes)
Q10 friend, co-worker (all the others are relatives)

Test 5 Complete the Sum

Q1 9
Q2 28
Q3 5
Q4 42
Q5 7
Q6 4
Q7 7
Q8 12
Q9 10
Q10 17

Test 6 Synonyms

Q1 discuss, debate
Q2 dodge, avoid
Q3 idle, lazy
Q4 anxious, nervous
Q5 plume, feather
Q6 blossom, flower
Q7 exit, leave
Q8 cry, sob
Q9 enthusiastic, keen
Q10 downpour, rain

Test 7 Code Sets

Q1 7354

Q2 BOLT

Q3 7355

For questions 1–3, the number 5 appears in position three and four of the code 8355 and therefore must equate to a double letter at the end of the word so LL. The number 3 appears in the second position of two words so must equate to A. Therefore 8152 must equate to BOLT as it is the only word without an A in it. From BOLT we know that 8 equates to B and therefore 8355 must stand for BALL. 35 stands for AL but it cannot be CALL as it does not end in two letters the same; therefore 7354 must be CALF.

Q4 8753

Q5 ROAM

Q6 4713

For questions 4–6, the number 7 appears in position two so must equate to O. Three of the words have a last letter E and one of the words ends in M so the number 5 must equate to M as the others have 3 as their final letter. Therefore 4725 is the code for the word ROAM. 5 (letter M) also appears in the third position of 8753 so must equate to HOME (87 stands for HO). Therefore 8713 must be HOSE.

Q7 5139

Q8 REAR

Q9 7137

For questions 7–9, there are two words ending in 139 so that must equate to EAR. We know then that letter 9 stands for R so the code 9139 must equate to REAR and 9178 therefore must be the other word starting with R, REST. 5139 must be PEAR.

Test 8 Word Analogies

Q1 war, energy (the words are antonyms)

Q2 puppy, fawn (the words are the offspring of the animal)

Q3 March, November (the words are the preceding months)

Q4 snout, paw (the words name the equivalent part of the anatomy on an animal)

Q5 tomorrow, yesterday (tomorrow is a day in the future and yesterday is a day in the past)

Q6 Italy, Greece (the words are the countries in which the capital cities can be found)

Q7 skiing, swimming (the words are sports that can be done in each environment)

Q8 temperature, pressure (the words are the type of measurement displayed on the instrument)

Q9 fresh, cowardly (the words are antonyms)

Q10 red, blue (the words are the colour of the gemstones)

Test 9 Letter Connections

Q1 w (the four words are knew, wrong, snow, worry)

Q2 y (the four words are they, yawn, clay, yolk)

Q3 c (the four words are magic, cuddle, toxic, case)

Q4 t (the four words are heat, tank, bandit, train)

Q5 c (the four words are chic, clap, music, crab)

Q6 k (the four words are milk, knot, pink, kick)

Q7 n (the four words are gain, neck, chin, none)

Q8 p (the four words are wasp, pint, sleep, plug)

Q9 t (the four words are pant, time, east, tower)

Q10 w (the four words are claw, wire, below, win)

Test 10 Hidden Words

Q1 done (avocado next)

Q2 them (with emotion)

Q3 wash (know Ashley)

Q4 heat (the attic)

Q5 hear (lunch early)

Q6 less (pineapples should)

Q7 path (top athletes)

Q8 till (until Lenny)

Q9 toad (photo adoringly)

Q10 tiny (satin yoga)

Test 11 Code Pairs

Q1 WBTF (+1, +1,+1,+1)

Q2 STATE (−7, +5, −3, +1, +0)

Q3 NIZ (−4, +4, −4)

Q4 TRAP (+3, −2, +3, −2)

Q5 JMHED (−1, −1, −1, −1, −1)

Q6 DIARY (+4, +0, −3, +0, +2)

Q7 QGYV (−2, +2, −2, +2)

Q8 BIRDS (−2, +3, −3, +2, −2)

Q9 XMKY (+1, −2, −4, −5)

Q10 RING (−1, +3, −5, +2)

Test 12 Problem Solving

Q1 **20**

32 cows; $\frac{1}{4}$ are Jersey cattle so $\frac{32}{4}$ = 8

Holstein cows = 32 − 8 = 24

$\frac{1}{6}$ of Holstein cows = 24 ÷ 6 = 4

Farmer Boggins has 24 − 4

= 20 Holstein cows

Q2 **4 days**

48 builders = 2 × 24 builders so it will take $\frac{1}{2}$ the time of 8 days = 4 days

Q3 **£18000**

£36000 − £6000 (Daniel) = £30000

Francis got $\frac{2}{5}$ of £30000 = £12000

Daniel + Francis got £6000 + £12000 = £18000

Q4 **8**

42 biscuits − 7 = 35 biscuits

Buster gets $\frac{1}{7}$ of 35 = 5 biscuits

30 biscuits − 14 biscuits = 16 biscuits

$\frac{1}{2}$ of 16 = 8 biscuits each for Buddy and Charlie

Q5 **Kerry**

Amber sits on the far left.

Davina sits between Kerry and Amber.

So Kerry sits on the far right.

Q6 **68**

Barry's grandmother is 5 × 12 (Barry's age) = 60; in 8 years she will be 60 + 8 = 68

Q7 **Sunday**

14th − 26th = 12 days

Tuesday + 12 days = Sunday

Q8 **84 eggs**

Eggs sold per day = 10 − 3 = 7

Eggs sold after 12 days = 7 × 12 = 84

Test 13 Letter Analogies

Q1 **ON** (1st letter +1, 2nd letter −1 OR reverse order of the two letters)

Q2 **HS** (1st letter +1, 2nd letter −1)

Q3 **VU** (1st letter +1, 2nd letter +1)

Q4 **TW** (1st letter −3, 2nd letter −3)

Q5 **UY** (1st letter +3, 2nd letter +0)

Q6 **PL** (1st letter +3, 2nd letter +3)

Q7 **LX** (1st letter +0, 2nd letter +2)

Q8 **QN** (1st letter −3, 2nd letter −3)

Q9 **WM** (1st letter +5, 2nd letter −5)

Q10 **JI** (1st letter −1, 2nd letter −1)

Test 14 Letters for Numbers

Q1 E

Q2 D

Q3 D

Q4 A

Q5 C

Q6 B

Q7 B

Q8 A

Q9 C

Q10 A

Test 15 Number Sequences

Q1 **17** (the sequence is +2)

Q2 **8** (the sequence is −3)

Q3 **9** (the sequence is −2, −1, −2, −1, −2)

Q4 **16** (the sequence is +3, −2, +3, −2, +3)

Q5 **41** (the sequence is +5)

Q6 **38** (the sequence is +5, +10, +5 +10, +5)

Q7 **125** (the sequence is ÷2)

Q8 **49** (the sequence is 12^2, 11^2, 10^2, 9^2, 8^2, 7^2)

Q9 **46** (the sequence is +6)

Q10 **17** (the sequence is −5, +4, −5, +4, −5)

Test 16 Move a Letter

Q1 **i** (the two new words are **run** and **sta_i_r**)

Q2 **l** (the two new words are **beach** and **p_l_an**)

Q3 **n** (the two new words are **crow** and **tow_n_**)

Q4 **t** (the two new words are **rain** and **pun_t_**)

Q5 **b** (the two new words are **rain** and **_b_each**)

Q6 **r** (the two new words are **font** and **_r_oar**)

Test 16 answers continue on next page

Q7 k (the two new words are **now** and **as_k_**)

Q8 m (the two new words are **tie** and **_m_arch**)

Q9 t (the two new words are **ramp** and **sigh_t_**)

Q10 l (the two new words are **food** and **s_l_ash**)

Test 17 Word Construction

Q1 **nest** (word one letter 3, word one letter 4, word two letter 4, word two letter 3)

Q2 **drab** (word two letter 4, word two letter 3, word two letter 2, word one letter 1)

Q3 **coat** (word one letter 1, word two letter 2, word one letter 3, word two letter 3)

Q4 **test** (word one letter 3, word one letter 4, word two letter 1, word two letter 2)

Q5 **rate** (word one letter 4, word one letter 2, word two letter 1, word two letter 3)

Q6 **sole** (word two letter 3, word one letter 2, word one letter 3, word one letter 4)

Q7 **obey** (word one letter 3, word one letter 1, word two letter 2, word two letter 1)

Q8 **frog** (word one letter 4, word two letter 1, word two letter 2, word one letter 1)

Q9 **grab** (word one letter 1, word one letter 4, word two letter 3, word two letter 4)

Q10 **heel** (word one letter 1, word one letter 2, word two letter 2, word two letter 3)

Test 18 Word Combinations

Q1 nobody (_no_ and _body_)

Q2 photocopy (_photo_ and _copy_)

Q3 skyscraper (_sky_ and _scraper_)

Q4 feather (_feat_ and _her_)

Q5 download (_down_ and _load_)

Q6 upset (_up_ and _set_)

Q7 forget (_for_ and _get_)

Q8 household (_house_ and _hold_)

Q9 extraordinary (_extra_ and _ordinary_)

Q10 strawberries (_straw_ and _berries_)

Test 19 Double Meanings

Q1 **like**
When used as a verb, like is a synonym of enjoy and love. When used as an adjective, like is a synonym of similar and resembling.

Q2 **close**
When used as an adjective, close is a synonym of near and adjacent. When used as a verb (with a different pronunciation), one sense of close is a synonym of shut and lock.

Q3 **watch**
When used as a verb, watch is a synonym of observe and look. When used as a noun, one sense of watch is a synonym of clock and timepiece.

Q4 **sink**
When used as a verb, sink is a synonym of drop and fall. When used as a noun, sink is a synonym of basin and bowl.

Q5 **minute**
When used as an adjective, minute is a synonym of tiny and little. When used as a noun (with a different pronunciation), minute is a measurement of time as are moment and second.

Q6 **stick**
When used as a noun, stick is a synonym of rod and twig. When used as a verb, one sense of stick is a synonym of fasten and glue.

Q7 **save**
When used as a verb, save is a synonym of keep and preserve as well as rescue and aid.

Q8 **fine**
When used as a noun, fine is a synonym of penalty and punishment. When used as an adjective, one sense of fine is a synonym of acceptable and reasonable.

Q9 **flat**
When used as an adjective, one sense of flat is a synonym of even and uniform. When used as a noun, one sense of flat is a synonym of apartment and penthouse.

Q10 **row**
When used as a noun, row is a synonym of line and column. Pronounced differently, it is also a synonym of argument and squabble.

Test 20 Related Numbers

a = the first number within the group of 3

b = the third number within the group of 3

Q1 **49** = (a × b) **= 7 × 7**

Q2 **14** = (a − b) **= 23 − 9**

Q3 **35** = (a + b) **= 22 + 13**

Q4 **63** = (b − a) **= 86 − 23**

Q5 $21 = (b \div a) = \mathbf{63 \div 3}$

Q6 $25 = (a + b) + 8 = \mathbf{(7 + 10) + 8}$

Q7 $16 = (a + b) - 6 = \mathbf{(14 + 8) - 6}$

Q8 $30 = (a \times b) + 2 = \mathbf{(4 \times 7) + 2}$

Q9 $36 = (a - b)^2 = \mathbf{(8 - 2)^2}$

Q10 $61 = (a - b) + 1 = \mathbf{(80 - 20) + 1}$

Test 21 Code Sequences

Q1 **VD** (1st letter: +2, +0, +2, +0, +2, 2nd letter: +2)

Q2 **BI** (1st letter: +1, 2nd letter: −2)

Q3 **MO** (1st letter: +2, 2nd letter: +2)

Q4 **FP** (1st letter: +1, 2nd letter: −2)

Q5 **VU** (1st letter: every other letter +1, 2nd letter: +0)

Q6 **RL** (1st letter: +5, −4, +3, −2, +1, 2nd letter: −1, +2, −3, +4, −5)

Q7 **YR** (1st letter: +1, 2nd letter: +2)

Q8 **AE** (1st letter: −1, 2nd letter: −2)

Q9 **HT** (1st letter: −3, 2nd letter: +3, −2, +3, −2, +3)

Q10 **IS** (1st letter: −1, 2nd letter: +1)

Test 22 Missing Letters

Q1 **AIR** (the word in capitals is STAIRCASE)

Q2 **TAN** (the word in capitals is UNDERSTAND)

Q3 **TOE** (the word in capitals is TOMATOES)

Q4 **PIT** (the word in capitals is CAPITAL)

Q5 **KEY** (the word in capitals is MONKEY)

Q6 **LAP** (the word in capitals is COLLAPSED)

Q7 **TIN** (the word in capitals is WRITING)

Q8 **KIN** (the word in capitals is BAKING)

Q9 **COP** (the word in capitals is HELICOPTER)

Q10 **ROT** (the word in capitals is PARROT)

Test 23 Antonyms

Q1 correct, wrong

Q2 enormous, tiny

Q3 always, never

Q4 wicked, good

Q5 failure, success

Q6 fascinating, dull

Q7 simple, complicated

Q8 dark, light

Q9 clean, dirty

Q10 dumb, intelligent

Test 24 Related Words

Q1 nail, builder (all the others are tools)

Q2 trousers, shirt (all the others are types of material)

Q3 caterpillar, dog (all the others are types of bird)

Q4 soft, birds (all the others are things that grow on animal skin)

Q5 shore, sand (all the others are types of tree)

Q6 comfortable, bed (all the others are types of chair)

Q7 cow, bear (all the others are types of young animal)

Q8 sour, phenomenal (all the others are synonyms of chunky/large)

Q9 sailor, wave (all the others are types of boat)

Q10 boots, shoes (all the others are types of measurement)

Test 25 Complete the Sum

Q1 6

Q2 11

Q3 13

Q4 8

Q5 2

Q6 29

Q7 11

Q8 23

Q9 19

Q10 10

Test 26 Synonyms

Q1 arid, dry

Q2 purchase, buy

Q3 myth, fable

Q4 vast, huge

Q5 odour, smell

Q6 happiness, joy

Test 26 answers continue on next page

Q7 mischievous, naughty

Q8 timid, shy

Q9 danger, peril

Q10 aid, help

Test 27 Code Sets

Q1 5893

Q2 WISH

Q3 6239

For questions 1–3, the number 8 appears in position four for two of the words so must equate to H. Number 8 (H) is the second letter of the code 5893 so this must be CHEF. F therefore must equate to the number 3. 3278 must be FISH and 6278 must be WISH.

Q4 7438

Q5 NEST

Q6 2943

For questions 4–6, the number 7 appears in position one for two of the words so it must equate to B. The numbers 43 appear twice in positions two and three so must equate to AR; therefore 8529 cannot be STAR and must equate to NEST. The number 8 equates to N so 7438 must equate to BARN.

Q7 8344

Q8 LIME

Q9 8347

For questions 7–9, the number 4 appears in the third and fourth position of the code 8344 so it must equate to L and the word must be MILL. If 4 = L then 4387 is LIME. As M is the number 8, 6348 must equate to FILM.

Test 28 Word Analogies

Q1 downcast, essential (the words are synonyms)

Q2 kitchen, classroom (the words are rooms in which the professional works)

Q3 hurl, alter (the words are synonyms)

Q4 sand, trees (the words are a common feature of the landscapes)

Q5 hide, scales (the words are the skin of the animals)

Q6 continent, city (the words are the type of geographical area that the place is)

Q7 fruit, meat (the words are the food categories that the food belongs to)

Q8 lay, sold (the words are the past tense of the original word)

Q9 historical, accidental (the words are the adjectives from the nouns)

Q10 miraculous, unbearable (the words are synonyms)

Test 29 Letter Connections

Q1 t (the four words are host, tour, shot, target)

Q2 f (the four words are leaf, fold, wolf, fist)

Q3 h (the four words are much, heel, both, hold)

Q4 r (the four words are near, rose, scar, reason)

Q5 g (the four words are sing, gate, mug, gang)

Q6 r (the four words are pear, rice, roar, race)

Q7 n (the four words are tin, nest, satin, newt)

Q8 m (the four words are prom, mouse, farm, male)

Q9 h (the four words are wash, hall, ranch, heat)

Q10 d (the four words are child, dime, band, door)

Test 30 Hidden Words

Q1 rash (Laura showed)

Q2 mice (mimic every)

Q3 near (within earshot)

Q4 bees (Maybe escaping)

Q5 spot (peels potatoes)

Q6 card (vicar decided)

Q7 than (month, another)

Q8 wink (threw inks)

Q9 epic (the picnic)

Q10 tall (Dermot allowed)

Test 31 Code Pairs

Q1 BOAT (−2, −3, −1, −4)

Q2 YFCN (+5, +5, +5, +5)

Q3 UUUZQE (+5, +0, −5, +0, +5,+0)

Q4 SELL (−3, +1, −3, +1)

Q5 JWIDO (+6, +5, +4, +3, +2)

Q6 AFKJJ (−3, +1, −3, +1, −3)

Q7 CAST (all the letters are reversed apart from the first letter of the word which moves one space back)

Q8 HATE (−2, −3, −2, −3)

Q9 UCOG (+5, − 6, +3, +2)

Q10 RAIN (+1, +1, +2, +2)

Test 32 Problem Solving

Q1 **6 chocolate bars**

£5.10 − £2.40 = £2.70 to buy chocolate bars

£2.70 ÷ £0.45 = 6 bars

Q2 **8**

Mandy (22) is twice the age of Rachel so

Rachel = 11; Vivian is three years younger

than Rachel = 8

Q3 **£27**

$\frac{2}{4} = \frac{1}{2} + \frac{1}{3} = \frac{3}{6} + \frac{2}{6} = \frac{5}{6}$ spent so $\frac{1}{6}$ remaining

$\frac{1}{6}$ = £4.50

Total = £4.50 × 6 = £27

Q4 **4.12 pm**

15 stops × 3 minutes each stop = 45 minutes

Bus leaves at 3.27 pm + 45 minutes so arrives

at 4.12 pm

Q5 **1.55 pm**

Real time = 1.45 pm (1.30 pm + 15 minutes)

Francis's watch is 10 minutes fast

so 10 minutes + 1.45 pm = 1.55 pm

Q6 **7 pm**

Mrs Williams' journey takes 45 minutes

Mrs Green's journey takes 4 × 45 minutes =

180 minutes = 3 hours

4 pm + 3 hours = 7 pm

Q7 **5 kg**

54 kg − Dog A (22 kg) − Dog B (15 kg) =

17 kg (weight of Dog C)

Dog A − Dog C = 22 − 17 = 5 kg difference

Q8 **24**

Alexander is 8 now (10 − 2)

Sue's age = 3 × 8 = 24

Test 33 Letter Analogies

Q1 **FD** (1st letter +4, 2nd letter +4)

Q2 **QY** (1st letter −4, 2nd letter +9)

Q3 **QV** (1st letter +4, 2nd letter +4)

Q4 **CV** (1st letter +6, 2nd letter −5)

Q5 **KV** (1st letter +4, 2nd letter −7)

Q6 **LP** (1st letter +7, 2nd letter +7)

Q7 **GY** (1st letter −5, 2nd letter +8)

Q8 **QO** (1st letter +2, 2nd letter +2)

Q9 **TT** (1st letter +2, 2nd letter +1)

Q10 **RF** (1st letter +2, 2nd letter −7)

Test 34 Letters for Numbers

Q1 E

Q2 B

Q3 B

Q4 D

Q5 C

Q6 A

Q7 A

Q8 C

Q9 E

Q10 A

Test 35 Number Sequences

Q1 **− 25** (the sequence is −15)

Q2 **107** (the sequence is −6 for the 1st, 3rd and 5th numbers and +4 for the 2nd, 4th and 6th numbers)

Q3 **14** (the sequence is +4, −1, +4, −1, +4)

Q4 **54** (the sequence for the 1st, 3rd and 5th numbers is +10 and the sequence for the 2nd, 4th and 6th numbers is −9)

Q5 **24** (the sequence is −6, +20, −12, +26, −18)

Q6 **33** (the sequence is +4)

Q7 **17** (the sequence is −3)

Q8 **25** (the sequence is +12, −9, + 6, −3, +0)

Q9 **77** (the sequence is +12)

Q10 **19** (the sequence is +3, +2, +3, +2, +3)

Test 36 Move a Letter

Q1 **i** (the two new words are **nose** and **ideal**)

Q2 **f** (the two new words are **lower** and **scarf**)

Q3 **c** (the two new words are **lock** and **crow**)

Q4 **b** (the two new words are **rake** and **bowl**)

Q5 **y** (the two new words are **must** and **busy**)

Q6 **s** (the two new words are **cure** and **stone** OR **tones**)

Test 36 answers continue on next page

Q7 r (the two new words are **gown** and **pray**)

Q8 h (the two new words are **our** and **thick**)

Q9 e (the two new words are **hard** and **every**)

Q10 o (the two new words are **sap** and **moat**)

Test 37 Word Construction

Q1 **sand** (word two letter 4, word two letter 2, word one letter 4, word one letter 1)

Q2 **king** (word two letter 4, word one letter 2, word one letter 3, word two letter 1)

Q3 **huge** (word two letter 1, word one letter 3, word two letter 4, word one letter 4)

Q4 **mist** (word two letter 4, word one letter 2, word two letter 1, word one letter 3)

Q5 **folk** (word two letter 1, word two letter 2, word one letter 3, word one letter 4)

Q6 **dens** (word two letter 2, word two letter 4, word one letter 3, word one letter 1)

Q7 **band** (word one letter 1, word two letter 3, word one letter 3, word two letter 1)

Q8 **boar** (word two letter 1, word two letter 3, word one letter 3, word one letter 1)

Q9 **army** (word two letter 2, word two letter 3, word two letter 4, word one letter 3)

Q10 **tune** (word one letter 4, word two letter 2, word one letter 3, word two letter 4)

Test 38 Word Combinations

Q1 seagull (sea and gull)

Q2 database (data and base)

Q3 handsome (hand and some)

Q4 format (for and mat)

Q5 lifetime (life and time)

Q6 island (is and land)

Q7 undergrowth (under and growth)

Q8 damage (dam and age)

Q9 buttercup (butter and cup)

Q10 eardrum (ear and drum)

Test 39 Double Meanings

Q1 **spring**
When used as a verb, spring is a synonym of leap and jump. When used as a noun, spring is a season (as are summer and autumn).

Q2 **light**
When used as a noun, one sense of light is a synonym of lamp and illumination. When used as an adjective, one sense of light is a synonym of bright and sunny.

Q3 **lie**
When used as a verb, one sense of lie is a synonym of recline and sprawl. When used as a noun, lie is a synonym of falsehood and deceit.

Q4 **bark**
When used as a verb, bark is similar in meaning to howl and yelp. When used as a noun, bark is a synonym of covering and skin.

Q5 **tear**
When used as a verb, tear is a synonym of split and rip. When used as a noun, tear is a synonym of drop and bead.

Q6 **match**
When used as a verb, match is a synonym of correspond and equal. When used as a noun, one sense of match is a synonym of contest and game.

Q7 **hide**
When used as a verb, hide is a synonym of conceal and bury. When used as a noun, one sense of hide is a synonym of pelt and skin.

Q8 **trip**
When used as a verb, one sense of trip is a synonym of slip and stumble. When used as a noun, one sense of trip is a synonym of excursion and journey.

Q9 **bow**
When used as a verb, bow is similar to nod and curtsy. When used as a noun (with a different pronunciation), bow is a synonym of knot and loop.

Q10 **kind**
When used as an adjective, kind is a synonym of considerate and loving. When used as a noun, kind is a synonym of sort and type.

Test 40 Related Numbers

a = the first number within the group of 3

b = the third number within the group of 3

Q1 $15 = (a \div b)$ **$= 60 \div 4$**

Q2 $68 = 2(a + b)$ **$= 2(14 + 20)$**

Q3 $6 = (a - b) \div 2$ **$= (45 - 33) \div 2$**

Q4 $65 = (a + b) + 10$ **$= (24 + 31) + 10$**

Q5 $55 = (a + b) = 36 + 19$
Q6 $40 = (a + 2b) = 2 + (2 \times 19)$
Q7 $49 = (a - b) = (82 - 33)$
Q8 $72 = 2 (a \times b) = 2 (36)$
Q9 $73 = (3a - b) = (75 - 2)$
Q10 $15 = (b - a) - 1 = (45 - 29) - 1$

Test 41 Code Sequences

Q1 **LN** (1st letter: +3, 2nd letter: −3, +4, −3, +4, −3)

Q2 **TO** (1st letter: every other term −1, −2, −1, −2, 2nd letter: +1)

Q3 **UO** (1st letter: +3, −3, +2, −2, +1, 2nd letter: −2)

Q4 **QJ** (1st letter: −1, 2nd letter: +9, −9, +7, −7, +5)

Q5 **EM** (1st letter: +0, −1, +2, −3, +4, 2nd letter: +0, −1, 0, −1, +0)

Q6 **ST** (1st letter: +3, −3, +3, −3, +3, 2nd letter: −2)

Q7 **JM** (1st letter: +1, +2, +1, +2, +1, 2nd letter: +1, −1, +2, −2, +3)

Q8 **FT** (1st letter: −2, 2nd letter: +1)

Q9 **OD** (1st letter: +2, +0, +2, +0, +2, 2nd letter: −1)

Q10 **PM** (1st letter: +1, 2nd letter: −1)

Test 42 Missing Letters

Q1 **ELM** (the word in capitals is HELMET)
Q2 **MAD** (the word in capitals is HOMEMADE)
Q3 **TAR** (the word in capitals is MUSTARD)
Q4 **RUB** (the word in capitals is RUBBISH)
Q5 **CAN** (the word in capitals is VOLCANO)
Q6 **NET** (the word in capitals is NINETY)
Q7 **OIL** (the word in capitals is BOILING)
Q8 **INN** (the word in capitals is DINNER)
Q9 **WAR** (the word in capitals is WARDROBE)
Q10 **ARK** (the word in capitals is SUPERMARKET)

Test 43 Antonyms

Q1 reward, punish
Q2 capture, release
Q3 first, last
Q4 deny, confirm
Q5 shrink, grow
Q6 certain, doubtful

Q7 minimum, maximum
Q8 rapid, slow
Q9 blunt, sharp
Q10 neat, untidy

Test 44 Related Words

Q1 liner, sea (all the others are types of hat)
Q2 place, meeting (all the others are types of fish)
Q3 spot, ease (all the others are synonyms of make good)
Q4 house, bed (all the others are rooms in a house)
Q5 delighted, bleak (all the others are synonyms of interested)
Q6 fall, slippery (all the others are words that refer to a journey)
Q7 guitar, violin (all the others are types of musical composition)
Q8 school, blackboard (all the others are types of bag)
Q9 paintbrush, artist (all the others are synonyms of illustration)
Q10 apprentice, student (all the others are types of profession)

Test 45 Complete the Sum

Q1 8
Q2 6
Q3 12
Q4 9
Q5 6
Q6 100
Q7 22
Q8 18
Q9 6
Q10 1

Test 46 Synonyms

Q1 vacant, empty
Q2 answer, response
Q3 perfume, fragrance
Q4 limb, leg

Test 46 answers continue on next page

Q5 concern, worry

Q6 comprehend, understand

Q7 ritual, habit

Q8 river, stream

Q9 affection, fondness

Q10 spade, shovel

Test 47 Code Sets

Q1 3761

Q2 TRIP

Q3 1637

For questions 1–3, the number 1 appears in position four of two of the codes so must equate to P. The number 7 is in the second position of two codes and in the first position of one of the codes so must equate to T. Therefore 7281 is TRIP. 3765 is STEM and 3761 is STEP because it ends in the number 1.

Q4 9792

Q5 KNOT

Q6 6792

For questions 4–6, the number 9 appears in the first and third position of the code 9792 so it must be the word NONE. 4975 has the letter N as the second letter so it must be KNOT. Therefore the number 5 equates to T so 5786 must be TOMB.

Q7 2663

Q8 MOTH

Q9 3665

For questions 7–9, the number 3 appears in position four of two of the words and must therefore equate to D. The number 6 appears in position two and three of two of the words so must equate to OO. Therefore 5612 equates to MOTH and the number 2 is H. So HOOD must equate to 2663.

Test 48 Word Analogies

Q1 endure, allow (the words are synonyms)

Q2 cure, logical (the words are synonyms)

Q3 length, direction (the words are values that are measured by the instruments)

Q4 end, help (the words are synonyms)

Q5 unlikely, punctual (the words are antonyms)

Q6 boat, clothes (the words are synonyms)

Q7 gallon, yard (the words are a larger measurement than the measurement value in bold)

Q8 bricks, metal (the words are the materials which form the structure of the item)

Q9 boring, illumination (the words are synonyms)

Q10 water, air (the words are the element absorbed/ingested by the action)

Test 49 Letter Connections

Q1 k (the four words are mask, kiss, rock, keep)

Q2 g (the four words are rug, gift, wring, grain)

Q3 d (the four words are food, dust, mood, dear)

Q4 c (the four words are manic, crop, public, cows)

Q5 e (the four words are inhale, enjoy, argue, eggs)

Q6 h (the four words are such, hound, peach, hand)

Q7 t (the four words are duet, task, lift, tar)

Q8 r (the four words are four, raft, hair, rest)

Q9 m (the four words are slam, moor, item, mail)

Q10 b (the four words are lamb, bold, stab, brain)

Test 50 Hidden Words

Q1 land (A**llan d**id)

Q2 date (pan**da te**nderly)

Q3 mess (beco**mes s**oggy)

Q4 bean (bathro**be an**d)

Q5 cold (fantasti**c, old**)

Q6 chin (Whi**ch in**strument)

Q7 here (teac**her e**ventually)

Q8 wasp (Fad**wa sp**ent)

Q9 meat (the**m eat**ing)

Q10 cart (side**car t**emperature)

Test 51 Code Pairs

Q1 LACE (−1, +3, −2, +2)

Q2 OLD (−8, −5, −3)

Q3 KQMC (−3, −2, +3, +2)

Q4 ZCWR (+3, +2, +4, +2)

Q5 THREE (+0, −5, +0, +5, +0)

Q6 FLNNY (−2, −3, −4, −5, −6)

Q7 DICE (−3, −1, −3, −1)

Q8 IBAF (+1, +1, +1, +1)

Q9 MAN (+10, +10, +10)

Q10 NNLXR (−5, +6, −3, −7, −1)

Test 52 Problem Solving

Q1 **1 hour 25 minutes**

Train journey = 7.52 am to 8.57 am =
1 hour 5 minutes

Richard's drive = 16 minutes + 4 minutes to
buy a ticket = 20 minutes

Total journey = 1 hour 5 minutes +
20 minutes = 1 hour 25 minutes

Q2 **6**

Louise is 12 now (in 7 years, she will be 19)
Katie is 4 now (Louise = 3 × Katie's age)

In two years Katie will be 6

Q3 **Friday**

4 days after tomorrow = 5 days after today

Today = Saturday so yesterday = Friday

Q4 **4.01 pm**

Real time = 4.28 pm − 15 minutes (Simon's
watch = 15 minutes fast) = 4.13 pm

My clock is 12 minutes slow = 4.01 pm

Q5 **16 pandas**

72 = 36 × 2

Therefore number of pandas = 8 × 2 = 16

Q6 **2 hours 15 minutes**

Nick leaves at 6.15 pm (45 minutes after Max
at 5.30 pm)

Joanne arrives at 8.30 pm (8 pm + 30 minutes)

Nick's journey time = 8.30 pm − 6.15 pm =
2 hours 15 minutes

Q7 **9 kg**

76 kg − Wolf A (31 kg) − Wolf B (18 kg) =
27 kg (weight of Wolf C)

Wolf C − Wolf B = 27 − 18 = 9 kg difference
in weight

Q8 **7.18 am**

Usually leave at 7.35 am (25 minutes to get
to school)

17 minutes before 7.35 am = 7.18 am

Test 53 Letter Analogies

Q1 **OP** (1st letter +9, 2nd letter +9)

Q2 **QM** (1st letter +3, 2nd letter −6)

Q3 **KM** (1st letter +1, 2nd letter +1)

Q4 **RA** (1st letter −2, 2nd letter +3)

Q5 **QV** (1st letter +2, 2nd letter +2)

Q6 **SO** (1st letter +9, 2nd letter +9)

Q7 **TO** (1st letter −3, 2nd letter −3)

Q8 **OV** (1st letter −1, 2nd letter +2)

Q9 **GH** (1st letter −6, 2nd letter −6)

Q10 **TX** (1st letter +5, 2nd letter +5)

Test 54 Letters for Numbers

Q1 B

Q2 C

Q3 D

Q4 D

Q5 A

Q6 D

Q7 B

Q8 C

Q9 E

Q10 E

Test 55 Number Sequences

Q1 **4** (the sequence is 7^2, 6^2, 5^2, 4^2, 3^2, 2^2)

Q2 **−1** (the sequence is +2, −4, +2, −4, +2)

Q3 **1** (the sequence is +1, −2, +1, −2, +1)

Q4 **0** (the sequence is −15)

Q5 **606** (the sequence is +101)

Q6 **138** (the sequence is +3, +5, +7, +9, +11)

Q7 **64** (the sequence is ×2)

Q8 **4** (the sequence is −2, +3, −2, +3, −2)

Q9 **213** (the sequence is +30)

Q10 **12** (the sequence is −17)

Test 56 Move a Letter

Q1 **g** (the two new words are **rub** and **thing**)

Q2 **c** (the two new words are **heap** and **score**)

Q3 **t** (the two new words are **cue** and **tread**)

Test 56 answers continue on next page

Test 56 answers continue on next page

Q4 c (the two new words are **loud** and **bat<u>c</u>h**)

Q5 a (the two new words are **pint** and **be<u>a</u>st**)

Q6 t (the two new words are **weigh** and **s<u>t</u>eal**)

Q7 b (the two new words are **land** and **<u>b</u>lame**)

Q8 r (the two new words are **fist** and **b<u>r</u>ass**)

Q9 d (the two new words are **fun** and **<u>d</u>rain**)

Q10 n (the two new words are **kit** and **brow<u>n</u>**)

Test 57 Word Construction

Q1 **tram** (word one letter 4, word two letter 1, word two letter 2, word one letter 1)

Q2 **move** (word two letter 1, word one letter 1, word one letter 2, word two letter 2)

Q3 **snow** (word one letter 3, word one letter 1, word two letter 2, word two letter 1)

Q4 **lace** (word two letter 2, word two letter 1, word one letter 1, word one letter 4)

Q5 **face** (word one letter 4, word two letter 2, word one letter 1, word two letter 4)

Q6 **line** (word one letter 4, word one letter 1, word two letter 5, word two letter 1)

Q7 **play** (word two letter 1, word one letter 3, word two letter 3, word one letter 1)

Q8 **call** (word one letter 1, word one letter 2, word one letter 3, word two letter 1)

Q9 **blue** (word two letter 3, word one letter 1, word two letter 2, word two letter 4)

Q10 **wand** (word two letter 1, word two letter 2, word one letter 1, word one letter 4)

Test 58 Word Combinations

Q1 pullover (<u>pull</u> and <u>over</u>)

Q2 counteract (<u>counter</u> and <u>act</u>)

Q3 password (<u>pass</u> and <u>word</u>)

Q4 friendship (<u>friend</u> and <u>ship</u>)

Q5 rather (<u>rat</u> and <u>her</u>)

Q6 behind (<u>be</u> and <u>hind</u>)

Q7 install (<u>in</u> and <u>stall</u>)

Q8 season (<u>sea</u> and <u>son</u>)

Q9 wholesome (<u>whole</u> and <u>some</u>)

Q10 sunlight (<u>sun</u> and <u>light</u>)

Test 59 Double Meanings

Q1 pen
When used as a noun, pen is a synonym of enclosure and hutch as well as marker and biro.

Q2 free
When used as an adjective, one sense of free is a synonym of complimentary and costless. When used as a verb, free is a synonym of release and liberate.

Q3 just
When used as an adverb, just is a synonym of only and merely. When used as an adjective, just is a synonym of lawful and fair.

Q4 lead
When used as a verb, lead is a synonym of guide and direct. When used as a noun (with a different pronunciation), lead is in the same category as metal and steel.

Q5 die
When used as a verb, die is a synonym of decease and perish. When used as a noun, die is a synonym of cube and counter.

Q6 present
When used as an adjective, present is a synonym of current and existing. When used as a noun, one sense of present is a synonym of gift and offering.

Q7 change
When used as a noun, change is a synonym of coins and money. When used as a verb, change is a synonym of transform and alter.

Q8 sign
When used as a noun, sign is a synonym of symbol and mark. When used as a verb, one sense of sign is a synonym of autograph and subscribe.

Q9 veil
When used as a noun, one sense of veil is a synonym of curtain and shroud. When used as a verb, veil is a synonym of conceal and hide.

Q10 rule
When used as a noun, rule is a synonym of regulation and law. When used as a verb, rule is a synonym of govern and reign.

Test 60 Related Numbers

a = the first number within the group of 3

b = the third number within the group of 3

Q1 $14 = (a \div b) + 2$ **= 96 ÷ 8 + 2**

Q2 $64 = (2a - b)$ **= 70 − 6**

Q3 $121 = (a + 1) \times b$ **= (10 + 1) × 11**

Q4 $17 = (a \times b) + 1$ **= (4 × 4) + 1**

Q5 $11 = (b \div a) - 1$ **= (96 ÷ 8) −1**

Q6 $15 = (b \div a) + 10$ **= (50 ÷ 10) + 10**

Q7 $16 = (a - b) - 3$ **= (38 − 19) − 3**

Q8 $48 = (a \times b)$ **= (6 × 8)**

Q9 $86 = (a^2 + b)$ **= 81 + 5**

Q10 $75 = (a - b)$ **= (81 − 6)**

Notes

ACKNOWLEDGEMENTS

The author and publisher are grateful to the copyright holders for permission to use quoted materials and images.

Every effort has been made to trace copyright holders and obtain their permission for the use of copyright material. The author and publisher will gladly receive information enabling them to rectify any error or omission in subsequent editions. All facts are correct at time of going to press.

Published by Collins
An imprint of HarperCollins*Publishers* Limited
1 London Bridge Street
London SE1 9GF

ISBN: 9781844199129

First published 2018

This edition published 2020

Previously published as Letts

10 9 8 7 6 5 4 3 2

British Library Cataloguing in Publication Data.

A CIP record of this book is available from the British Library.

Author: Flora MacInnes, a tutor for Bonas MacFarlane
Series Editor: Faisal Nasim
Commissioning Editor: Michelle I'Anson
Editor and Project Manager: Sonia Dawkins
Cover Design: Sarah Duxbury and Kevin Robbins
Text and Page Design: Ian Wrigley
Layout and Artwork: Q2A Media
Production: Natalia Rebow
Printed by CPI Group (UK) Ltd, Croydon CR0 4YY

MIX
Paper from
responsible source
FSC
www.fsc.org
FSC™ C007454

This book is produced from independently certified FSC™ paper to ensure responsible forest management.

For more information visit:
www.harpercollins.co.uk/green